THIS BOOK BELONGS TO:

_____

_____

Index

Index

Wine:

Vintage:

Grapes: _____

Type: _____

Region: _____

ABV: _____

Producer: _____

Serving Temp: _____

Pairs with: _____

Suggested Glass:

Price:	Purchased/Gift from:	Date Purchased/ Received:

Tasting

When:

Where:

With:

Overall Rating:

☆☆☆☆☆

Recommend?

(YES) (NO)

Description

Appearance: _____

Aroma: _____

Body: _____

Palate: _____

Finish: _____

Additional Notes/Comments

_____
_____
_____
_____
_____
_____
_____
_____

Wine:

Vintage:

Grapes: _____

Type: _____

Region: _____

ABV: _____

Producer: _____

Serving Temp: _____

Pairs with: _____

Suggested Glass:

Price:	Purchased/Gift from:	Date Purchased/Received:

Tasting

When: _____

Where: _____

With: _____

Overall Rating:

☆☆☆☆☆

Recommend?

(YES) (NO)

Description

Appearance: _____

Aroma: _____

Body: _____

Palate: _____

Finish: _____

Additional Notes/Comments

_____
_____
_____
_____
_____
_____
_____
_____
_____

Wine:

Vintage:

Grapes:

Type:

Region:

ABV:

Producer:

Serving Temp:

Pairs with:

Suggested Glass:

Price:	Purchased/Gift from:	Date Purchased/ Received:

Tasting

When:

Where:

With:

Overall Rating:

☆☆☆☆☆

Recommend?

YES   NO

Description

Appearance:

Aroma:

Body:

Palate:

Finish:

Additional Notes/Comments

Wine:

Vintage:

Grapes: _____

Type: _____

Region: _____

ABV: _____

Producer: _____

Serving Temp: _____

Pairs with: _____

Suggested Glass:

Price:	Purchased/Gift from:	Date Purchased/Received:

Tasting	Description

When:

Appearance: _____

Where:

Aroma: _____

With:

Body: _____

Overall Rating:

☆☆☆☆☆

Palate: _____

Recommend?

(YES) (NO)

Finish: _____

Additional Notes/Comments

_____
_____
_____
_____
_____
_____
_____
_____

Wine:

Vintage:

Grapes: _____

Region: _____

Producer: _____

Pairs with: _____

Type: _____

ABV: _____

Serving Temp: _____

Suggested Glass:

Price:	Purchased/Gift from:	Date Purchased/ Received:

Tasting

When:

Where:

With:

Overall Rating:

☆☆☆☆☆

Recommend?

(YES)   (NO)

Description

Appearance: _____

Aroma: _____

Body: _____

Palate: _____

Finish: _____

Additional Notes/Comments

_____
_____
_____
_____
_____
_____
_____

Wine:

Vintage:

Grapes:

Type:

Region:

ABV:

Producer:

Serving Temp:

Pairs with:

Suggested Glass:

Price:	Purchased/Gift from:	Date Purchased/ Received:

Tasting

When:

Where:

With:

Overall Rating:

☆☆☆☆☆

Recommend?

YES NO

Description

Appearance:

Aroma:

Body:

Palate:

Finish:

Additional Notes/Comments

Wine:

Vintage:

Grapes: _____

Type: _____

Region: _____

ABV: _____

Producer: _____

Serving Temp: _____

Pairs with: _____

Suggested Glass:

Price:	Purchased/Gift from:	Date Purchased/Received:

Tasting

When: _____

Where: _____

With: _____

Overall Rating:

☆☆☆☆☆

Recommend?

(YES)   (NO)

Description

Appearance: _____

Aroma: _____

Body: _____

Palate: _____

Finish: _____

Additional Notes/Comments

_____
_____
_____
_____
_____
_____
_____
_____

Wine:

Vintage:

Grapes: _____

Region: _____

Producer: _____

Pairs with: _____

Type: _____

ABV: _____

Serving Temp: _____

Suggested Glass:

Price:	Purchased/Gift from:	Date Purchased/Received:

Tasting

When: _____

Where: _____

With: _____

Overall Rating:

☆☆☆☆☆

Recommend?

(YES)   (NO)

Description

Appearance: _____

Aroma: _____

Body: _____

Palate: _____

Finish: _____

Additional Notes/Comments

_____
_____
_____
_____
_____
_____
_____
_____
_____

Wine:

Vintage:

Grapes: _____

Type: _____

Region: _____

ABV: _____

Producer: _____

Serving Temp: _____

Pairs with: _____

Suggested Glass:

Price:	Purchased/Gift from:	Date Purchased/ Received:

Tasting

When: _____

Where: _____

With: _____

Overall Rating:

☆☆☆☆☆

Recommend?

YES   NO

Description

Appearance: _____

Aroma: _____

Body: _____

Palate: _____

Finish: _____

Additional Notes/Comments

_____
_____
_____
_____
_____
_____
_____
_____

Wine:

Vintage:

Grapes:

Region:

Producer:

Pairs with:

Type:

ABV:

Serving Temp:

Suggested Glass:

Price:	Purchased/Gift from:	Date Purchased/ Received:

Tasting

When:

Where:

With:

Overall Rating:

☆☆☆☆☆

Recommend?

(YES) (NO)

Description

Appearance:

Aroma:

Body:

Palate:

Finish:

Additional Notes/Comments

Wine:

Vintage:

Grapes: _____

Type: _____

Region: _____

ABV: _____

Producer: _____

Serving Temp: _____

Pairs with: _____

Suggested Glass:

Price:	Purchased/Gift from:	Date Purchased/ Received:

Tasting

When:

Where:

With:

Overall Rating:

☆☆☆☆☆

Recommend?

YES   NO

Description

Appearance: _____

Aroma: _____

Body: _____

Palate: _____

Finish: _____

Additional Notes/Comments

_____
_____
_____
_____
_____
_____
_____
_____

Wine:

Vintage:

Grapes:

Region:

Producer:

Pairs with:

Type:

ABV:

Serving Temp:

Suggested Glass:

Price:	Purchased/Gift from:	Date Purchased/Received:

Tasting

When:

Where:

With:

Overall Rating:

☆☆☆☆☆

Recommend?

(YES) (NO)

Description

Appearance:

Aroma:

Body:

Palate:

Finish:

Additional Notes/Comments

Wine:

Vintage:

Grapes:

Type:

Region:

ABV:

Producer:

Serving Temp:

Pairs with:

Suggested Glass:

Price:	Purchased/Gift from:	Date Purchased/ Received:

Tasting

When:

Where:

With:

Description

Appearance:

Aroma:

Body:

Overall Rating:

☆☆☆☆☆

Palate:

Recommend?

YES   NO

Finish:

Additional Notes/Comments

Wine:

Vintage:

Grapes: _____

Region: _____

Producer: _____

Pairs with: _____

Type: _____

ABV: _____

Serving Temp: _____

Suggested Glass:

Price:	Purchased/Gift from:	Date Purchased/Received:

Tasting

When: _____

Where: _____

With: _____

Overall Rating:

☆☆☆☆☆

Recommend?

(YES)   (NO)

Description

Appearance: _____

_____

Aroma: _____

_____

Body: _____

_____

Palate: _____

_____

Finish: _____

_____

Additional Notes/Comments

_____
_____
_____
_____
_____
_____
_____
_____
_____
_____

Wine:

Vintage:

Grapes:

Type:

Region:

ABV:

Producer:

Serving Temp:

Pairs with:

Suggested Glass:

Price:	Purchased/Gift from:	Date Purchased/Received:

Tasting

Description

When:

Appearance:

Where:

Aroma:

With:

Body:

Overall Rating:

☆☆☆☆☆

Palate:

Recommend?

(YES) (NO)

Finish:

Additional Notes/Comments

Wine:

Vintage:

Grapes: _____

Type: _____

Region: _____

ABV: _____

Producer: _____

Serving Temp: _____

Pairs with: _____

Suggested Glass:

Price:	Purchased/Gift from:	Date Purchased/Received:

Tasting

When: _____

Where: _____

With: _____

Overall Rating:

☆☆☆☆☆

Recommend?

(YES) (NO)

Description

Appearance: _____

Aroma: _____

Body: _____

Palate: _____

Finish: _____

Additional Notes/Comments

_____
_____
_____
_____
_____
_____
_____
_____
_____

Wine:

Vintage:

Grapes: _____

Type: _____

Region: _____

ABV: _____

Producer: _____

Serving Temp: _____

Pairs with: _____

Suggested Glass:

Price:	Purchased/Gift from:	Date Purchased/Received:

Tasting	Description

When:

Appearance: _____

Where:

Aroma: _____

With:

Body: _____

Overall Rating:

☆☆☆☆☆

Palate: _____

Recommend?

YES   NO

Finish: _____

Additional Notes/Comments

_____
_____
_____
_____
_____
_____
_____
_____

Wine:

Vintage:

Grapes:

Type:

Region:

ABV:

Producer:

Serving Temp:

Pairs with:

Suggested Glass:

Price:	Purchased/Gift from:	Date Purchased/ Received:

Tasting

Description

When:

Appearance:

Where:

Aroma:

With:

Body:

Overall Rating:

☆☆☆☆☆

Palate:

Recommend?

(YES) (NO)

Finish:

Additional Notes/Comments

Wine:

Vintage:

Grapes:

Type:

Region:

ABV:

Producer:

Serving Temp:

Pairs with:

Suggested Glass:

Price:	Purchased/Gift from:	Date Purchased/Received:

Tasting

When:

Where:

With:

Overall Rating:

☆☆☆☆☆

Recommend?

YES　　NO

Description

Appearance:

Aroma:

Body:

Palate:

Finish:

Additional Notes/Comments

Wine:

Vintage:

Grapes: _____

Type: _____

Region: _____

ABV: _____

Producer: _____

Serving Temp: _____

Pairs with: _____

Suggested Glass:

Price:	Purchased/Gift from:	Date Purchased/Received:

Tasting

Description

When:

Appearance: _____

Where:

Aroma: _____

With:

Body: _____

Overall Rating:

☆☆☆☆☆

Palate: _____

Recommend?

(YES) (NO)

Finish: _____

Additional Notes/Comments

_____
_____
_____
_____
_____
_____
_____
_____
_____

Wine:

Vintage:

Grapes: _____

Type: _____

Region: _____

ABV: _____

Producer: _____

Serving Temp: _____

Pairs with: _____

Suggested Glass:

Price:	Purchased/Gift from:	Date Purchased/ Received:

Tasting

When:

Where:

With:

Overall Rating:

☆☆☆☆☆

Recommend?

(YES) (NO)

Description

Appearance: _____

Aroma: _____

Body: _____

Palate: _____

Finish: _____

Additional Notes/Comments

_____
_____
_____
_____
_____
_____
_____
_____

Wine:

Vintage:

Grapes:

Type:

Region:

ABV:

Producer:

Serving Temp:

Pairs with:

Suggested Glass:

Price:	Purchased/Gift from:	Date Purchased/Received:

Tasting

When:

Where:

With:

Overall Rating:

☆☆☆☆☆

Recommend?

YES   NO

Description

Appearance:

Aroma:

Body:

Palate:

Finish:

Additional Notes/Comments

Wine:

Vintage:

Grapes: _____

Type: _____

Region: _____

ABV: _____

Producer: _____

Serving Temp: _____

Pairs with: _____

Suggested Glass:

Price:	Purchased/Gift from:	Date Purchased/ Received:

Tasting	Description

When:

Appearance: _____

Where:

Aroma: _____

With:

Body: _____

Overall Rating:

☆☆☆☆☆

Palate: _____

Recommend?

YES NO

Finish: _____

Additional Notes/Comments

_____
_____
_____
_____
_____
_____
_____
_____

Wine:

Vintage:

Grapes:

Type:

Region:

ABV:

Producer:

Serving Temp:

Pairs with:

Suggested Glass:

Price:	Purchased/Gift from:	Date Purchased/Received:

Tasting

When:

Where:

With:

Overall Rating:

☆☆☆☆☆

Recommend?

YES   NO

Description

Appearance:

Aroma:

Body:

Palate:

Finish:

Additional Notes/Comments

Wine:

Vintage:

Grapes: _____

Type: _____

Region: _____

ABV: _____

Producer: _____

Serving Temp: _____

Pairs with: _____

Suggested Glass:

Price:	Purchased/Gift from:	Date Purchased/Received:

Tasting

When: ....

Where: ....

With:

Overall Rating:
☆☆☆☆☆

Recommend?

(YES)   (NO)

Description

Appearance: _____

Aroma: _____

Body: _____

Palate: _____

Finish: _____

Additional Notes/Comments

_____
_____
_____
_____
_____
_____
_____
_____

Wine:

Vintage:

Grapes:

Region:

Producer:

Pairs with:

Type:

ABV:

Serving Temp:

Suggested Glass:

Price:	Purchased/Gift from:	Date Purchased/Received:

Tasting

When:

Where:

With:

Overall Rating:

☆☆☆☆☆

Recommend?

YES   NO

Description

Appearance:

Aroma:

Body:

Palate:

Finish:

Additional Notes/Comments

Wine:

Vintage:

Grapes:

Type:

Region:

ABV:

Producer:

Serving Temp:

Pairs with:

Suggested Glass:

Price:	Purchased/Gift from:	Date Purchased/ Received:

Tasting

When:

Where:

With:

Overall Rating:

☆☆☆☆☆

Recommend?

YES   NO

Description

Appearance:

Aroma:

Body:

Palate:

Finish:

Additional Notes/Comments

Wine:

Vintage:

Grapes:

Type:

Region:

ABV:

Producer:

Serving Temp:

Pairs with:

Suggested Glass:

Price:	Purchased/Gift from:	Date Purchased/Received:

Tasting

When:

Where:

With:

Overall Rating:

☆☆☆☆☆

Recommend?

YES   NO

Description

Appearance:

Aroma:

Body:

Palate:

Finish:

Additional Notes/Comments

Wine:

Vintage:

Grapes: _____

Type: _____

Region: _____

ABV: _____

Producer: _____

Serving Temp: _____

Pairs with: _____

Suggested Glass:

Price:	Purchased/Gift from:	Date Purchased/ Received:

Tasting

When:

Where:

With:

Overall Rating:

☆☆☆☆☆

Recommend?

YES   NO

Description

Appearance: _____

Aroma: _____

Body: _____

Palate: _____

Finish: _____

Additional Notes/Comments

_____
_____
_____
_____
_____
_____
_____
_____

Wine:

Vintage:

Grapes: _____

Type: _____

Region: _____

ABV: _____

Producer: _____

Serving Temp: _____

Pairs with: _____

Suggested Glass:

Price:	Purchased/Gift from:	Date Purchased/Received:

Tasting

When: _____

Where: _____

With: _____

Overall Rating:

☆☆☆☆☆

Recommend?

(YES) (NO)

Description

Appearance: _____

Aroma: _____

Body: _____

Palate: _____

Finish: _____

Additional Notes/Comments

_____
_____
_____
_____
_____
_____
_____
_____
_____

Wine:

Vintage:

Grapes: _____

Type: _____

Region: _____

ABV: _____

Producer: _____

Serving Temp: _____

Pairs with: _____

Suggested Glass:

Price:	Purchased/Gift from:	Date Purchased/ Received:

Tasting	Description

When:

Appearance: _____

Where:

Aroma: _____

With:

Body: _____

Overall Rating:
☆☆☆☆☆

Palate: _____

Recommend?
(YES) (NO)

Finish: _____

Additional Notes/Comments

_____
_____
_____
_____
_____
_____
_____
_____

Wine:

Vintage:

Grapes:

Type:

Region:

ABV:

Producer:

Serving Temp:

Pairs with:

Suggested Glass:

Price:	Purchased/Gift from:	Date Purchased/Received:

Tasting

When:

Where:

With:

Description

Appearance:

Aroma:

Body:

Overall Rating:

☆☆☆☆☆

Palate:

Recommend?

YES   NO

Finish:

Additional Notes/Comments

Wine:

Vintage:

Grapes: _____

Type: _____

Region: _____

ABV: _____

Producer: _____

Serving Temp: _____

Pairs with: _____

Suggested Glass:

Price:	Purchased/Gift from:	Date Purchased/Received:

Tasting

When:

Where:

With:

Overall Rating:

☆☆☆☆☆

Recommend?

(YES) (NO)

Description

Appearance: _____

Aroma: _____

Body: _____

Palate: _____

Finish: _____

Additional Notes/Comments

_____
_____
_____
_____
_____
_____
_____
_____

Wine:

Vintage:

Grapes:

Type:

Region:

ABV:

Producer:

Serving Temp:

Pairs with:

Suggested Glass:

Price:	Purchased/Gift from:	Date Purchased/Received:

Tasting

When:

Where:

With:

Overall Rating:

☆☆☆☆☆

Recommend?

(YES) (NO)

Description

Appearance:

Aroma:

Body:

Palate:

Finish:

Additional Notes/Comments

Wine:

Vintage:

Grapes: _____

Type: _____

Region: _____

ABV: _____

Producer: _____

Serving Temp: _____

Pairs with: _____

Suggested Glass:

Price:	Purchased/Gift from:	Date Purchased/ Received:

Tasting

When: _____

Where: _____

With: _____

Overall Rating:

☆☆☆☆☆

Recommend?

YES   NO

Description

Appearance: _____

Aroma: _____

Body: _____

Palate: _____

Finish: _____

Additional Notes/Comments

_____
_____
_____
_____
_____
_____
_____
_____

Wine:

Vintage:

Grapes:

Type:

Region:

ABV:

Producer:

Serving Temp:

Pairs with:

Suggested Glass:

Price:	Purchased/Gift from:	Date Purchased/Received:

Tasting

When:

Where:

With:

Overall Rating:

☆☆☆☆☆

Recommend?

YES   NO

Description

Appearance:

Aroma:

Body:

Palate:

Finish:

Additional Notes/Comments

Wine:

Vintage:

Grapes:

Type:

Region:

ABV:

Producer:

Serving Temp:

Pairs with:

Suggested Glass:

Price:	Purchased/Gift from:	Date Purchased/Received:

Tasting

When:

Where:

With:

Overall Rating:
☆☆☆☆☆

Recommend?
(YES) (NO)

Description

Appearance:

Aroma:

Body:

Palate:

Finish:

Additional Notes/Comments

Wine:

Vintage:

Grapes:

Type:

Region:

ABV:

Producer:

Serving Temp:

Pairs with:

Suggested Glass:

Price:	Purchased/Gift from:	Date Purchased/ Received:

Tasting

When:

Where:

With:

Overall Rating:

☆☆☆☆☆

Recommend?

(YES) (NO)

Description

Appearance:

Aroma:

Body:

Palate:

Finish:

Additional Notes/Comments

Wine:

Vintage:

Grapes: _____

Type: _____

Region: _____

ABV: _____

Producer: _____

Serving Temp: _____

Pairs with: _____

Suggested Glass:

Price:	Purchased/Gift from:	Date Purchased/ Received:

Tasting

When: _____

Where: _____

With: _____

Overall Rating:

☆☆☆☆☆

Recommend?

(YES) (NO)

Description

Appearance: _____

Aroma: _____

Body: _____

Palate: _____

Finish: _____

Additional Notes/Comments

_____
_____
_____
_____
_____
_____
_____
_____

Wine:

Vintage:

Grapes:

Type:

Region:

ABV:

Producer:

Serving Temp:

Pairs with:

Suggested Glass:

Price:	Purchased/Gift from:	Date Purchased/Received:

Tasting

When:

Where:

With:

Overall Rating:

☆☆☆☆☆

Recommend?

(YES)   (NO)

Description

Appearance:

Aroma:

Body:

Palate:

Finish:

Additional Notes/Comments

Wine:

Vintage:

Grapes: _____

Type: _____

Region: _____

ABV: _____

Producer: _____

Serving Temp: _____

Pairs with: _____

Suggested Glass:

Price:	Purchased/Gift from:	Date Purchased/Received:

Tasting

When:

Where:

With:

Overall Rating:

☆☆☆☆☆

Recommend?

YES   NO

Description

Appearance: _____

Aroma: _____

Body: _____

Palate: _____

Finish: _____

Additional Notes/Comments

_____
_____
_____
_____
_____
_____
_____
_____

Wine:

Vintage:

Grapes:

Type:

Region:

ABV:

Producer:

Serving Temp:

Pairs with:

Suggested Glass:

Price:	Purchased/Gift from:	Date Purchased/ Received:

Tasting

When:

Where:

With:

Description

Appearance:

Aroma:

Body:

Overall Rating:

☆☆☆☆☆

Palate:

Recommend?

YES   NO

Finish:

Additional Notes/Comments

Wine:

Vintage:

Grapes: _____

Type: _____

Region: _____

ABV: _____

Producer: _____

Serving Temp: _____

Pairs with: _____

Suggested Glass:

Price:	Purchased/Gift from:	Date Purchased/ Received:

Tasting	Description
When:	Appearance:
Where:	Aroma:
With:	Body:

Overall Rating:
☆☆☆☆☆

Palate:

Recommend?
YES   NO

Finish:

Additional Notes/Comments

_____
_____
_____
_____
_____
_____
_____
_____

Wine:

Vintage:

Grapes:

Region:

Producer:

Pairs with:

Type:

ABV:

Serving Temp:

Suggested Glass:

Price:	Purchased/Gift from:	Date Purchased/Received:

Tasting

When:

Where:

With:

Overall Rating:
☆☆☆☆☆

Recommend?
YES   NO

Description

Appearance:

Aroma:

Body:

Palate:

Finish:

Additional Notes/Comments

Wine:

Vintage:

Grapes:

Type:

Region:

ABV:

Producer:

Serving Temp:

Pairs with:

Suggested Glass:

Price:	Purchased/Gift from:	Date Purchased/Received:

Tasting

When:

Where:

With:

Overall Rating:

☆☆☆☆☆

Recommend?

YES   NO

Description

Appearance:

Aroma:

Body:

Palate:

Finish:

Additional Notes/Comments

Wine:

Vintage:

Grapes:

Type:

Region:

ABV:

Producer:

Serving Temp:

Pairs with:

Suggested Glass:

Price:	Purchased/Gift from:	Date Purchased/ Received:

Tasting

When:

Where:

With:

Overall Rating:

☆☆☆☆☆

Recommend?

(YES) (NO)

Description

Appearance:

Aroma:

Body:

Palate:

Finish:

Additional Notes/Comments

Wine:

Vintage:

Grapes: _____

Type: _____

Region: _____

ABV: _____

Producer: _____

Serving Temp: _____

Pairs with: _____

Suggested Glass:

Price:	Purchased/Gift from:	Date Purchased/ Received:

Tasting

When:

Where:

With:

Overall Rating:
☆☆☆☆☆

Recommend?
YES   NO

Description

Appearance: _____

Aroma: _____

Body: _____

Palate: _____

Finish: _____

Additional Notes/Comments

_____
_____
_____
_____
_____
_____
_____
_____

Wine:

Vintage:

Grapes:

Type:

Region:

ABV:

Producer:

Serving Temp:

Pairs with:

Suggested Glass:

Price:	Purchased/Gift from:	Date Purchased/ Received:

Tasting

When:

Where:

With:

Overall Rating:

☆☆☆☆☆

Recommend?

(YES) (NO)

Description

Appearance:

Aroma:

Body:

Palate:

Finish:

Additional Notes/Comments

Wine:

Vintage:

Grapes: _____

Type: _____

Region: _____

ABV: _____

Producer: _____

Serving Temp: _____

Pairs with: _____

Suggested Glass:

Price:	Purchased/Gift from:	Date Purchased/Received:

Tasting

When:

Where:

With:

Overall Rating:
☆☆☆☆☆

Recommend?
YES   NO

Description

Appearance: _____

Aroma: _____

Body: _____

Palate: _____

Finish: _____

Additional Notes/Comments

_____
_____
_____
_____
_____
_____
_____
_____
_____

Wine:

Vintage:

Grapes:

Type:

Region:

ABV:

Producer:

Serving Temp:

Pairs with:

Suggested Glass:

Price:	Purchased/Gift from:	Date Purchased/Received:

Tasting

When:

Where:

With:

Overall Rating:

☆☆☆☆☆

Recommend?

(YES) (NO)

Description

Appearance:

Aroma:

Body:

Palate:

Finish:

Additional Notes/Comments

Wine:

Vintage:

Grapes: _____

Type: _____

Region: _____

ABV: _____

Producer: _____

Serving Temp: _____

Pairs with: _____

Suggested Glass:

Price:	Purchased/Gift from:	Date Purchased/Received:

Tasting

When: _____

Where: _____

With: _____

Overall Rating:

☆☆☆☆☆

Recommend?

(YES)   (NO)

Description

Appearance: _____

Aroma: _____

Body: _____

Palate: _____

Finish: _____

Additional Notes/Comments

_____
_____
_____
_____
_____
_____
_____
_____

Wine:

Vintage:

Grapes:

Type:

Region:

ABV:

Producer:

Serving Temp:

Pairs with:

Suggested Glass:

Price:	Purchased/Gift from:	Date Purchased/Received:

Tasting

When:

Where:

With:

Overall Rating:

☆☆☆☆☆

Recommend?

YES NO

Description

Appearance:

Aroma:

Body:

Palate:

Finish:

Additional Notes/Comments

Wine:

Vintage:

Grapes:

Type:

Region:

ABV:

Producer:

Serving Temp:

Pairs with:

Suggested Glass:

Price:	Purchased/Gift from:	Date Purchased/Received:

Tasting

When:

Where:

With:

Overall Rating:

☆☆☆☆☆

Recommend?

(YES)   (NO)

Description

Appearance:

Aroma:

Body:

Palate:

Finish:

Additional Notes/Comments

Wine:

Vintage:

Grapes:

Type:

Region:

ABV:

Producer:

Serving Temp:

Pairs with:

Suggested Glass:

Price:	Purchased/Gift from:	Date Purchased/Received:

Tasting

When:

Where:

With:

Overall Rating:

☆☆☆☆☆

Recommend?

YES   NO

Description

Appearance:

Aroma:

Body:

Palate:

Finish:

Additional Notes/Comments

Wine:

Vintage:

Grapes: _____

Type: _____

Region: _____

ABV: _____

Producer: _____

Serving Temp: _____

Pairs with: _____

Suggested Glass:

Price:	Purchased/Gift from:	Date Purchased/ Received:

Tasting

When:

Where:

With:

Overall Rating:

☆☆☆☆☆

Recommend?

(YES)   (NO)

Description

Appearance: _____

Aroma: _____

Body: _____

Palate: _____

Finish: _____

Additional Notes/Comments

_____
_____
_____
_____
_____
_____
_____
_____

Wine:

Vintage:

Grapes:

Type:

Region:

ABV:

Producer:

Serving Temp:

Pairs with:

Suggested Glass:

Price:	Purchased/Gift from:	Date Purchased/Received:

Tasting

Description

When:

Appearance:

Where:

Aroma:

With:

Body:

Overall Rating:
☆☆☆☆☆

Palate:

Recommend?

YES   NO

Finish:

Additional Notes/Comments

Wine:

Vintage:

Grapes: _____

Type: _____

Region: _____

ABV: _____

Producer: _____

Serving Temp: _____

Pairs with: _____

Suggested Glass:

Price:	Purchased/Gift from:	Date Purchased/ Received:
,		

Tasting

When:

Where:

With:

Overall Rating:
☆☆☆☆☆

Recommend?
YES   NO

Description

Appearance: _____

Aroma: _____

Body: _____

Palate: _____

Finish: _____

Additional Notes/Comments

_____
_____
_____
_____
_____
_____
_____
_____

Wine:

Vintage:

Grapes:

Type:

Region:

ABV:

Producer:

Serving Temp:

Pairs with:

Suggested Glass:

Price:	Purchased/Gift from:	Date Purchased/ Received:

Tasting

When:

Where:

With:

Overall Rating:

☆☆☆☆☆

Recommend?

(YES) (NO)

Description

Appearance:

Aroma:

Body:

Palate:

Finish:

Additional Notes/Comments

Wine:

Vintage:

Grapes:

Type:

Region:

ABV:

Producer:

Serving Temp:

Pairs with:

Suggested Glass:

Price: | **Purchased/Gift from:** | **Date Purchased/ Received:**

Tasting

When:

Where:

With:

Overall Rating:

☆☆☆☆☆

Recommend?

(YES) (NO)

Description

Appearance:

Aroma:

Body:

Palate:

Finish:

Additional Notes/Comments

Wine:

Vintage:

Grapes: _____

Type: _____

Region: _____

ABV: _____

Producer: _____

Serving Temp: _____

Pairs with: _____

Suggested Glass:

Price:	Purchased/Gift from:	Date Purchased/Received:

Tasting

When:

Where:

With:

Overall Rating:
☆☆☆☆☆

Recommend?
(YES)   (NO)

Description

Appearance: _____

Aroma: _____

Body: _____

Palate: _____

Finish: _____

Additional Notes/Comments

_____
_____
_____
_____
_____
_____
_____
_____
_____

Wine:

Vintage:

Grapes:

Type:

Region:

ABV:

Producer:

Serving Temp:

Pairs with:

Suggested Glass:

Price:	Purchased/Gift from:	Date Purchased/ Received:

Tasting

When:

Where:

With:

Overall Rating:

☆☆☆☆☆

Recommend?

(YES) (NO)

Description

Appearance:

Aroma:

Body:

Palate:

Finish:

Additional Notes/Comments

Wine:

Vintage:

Grapes:

Type:

Region:

ABV:

Producer:

Serving Temp:

Pairs with:

Suggested Glass:

Price:	Purchased/Gift from:	Date Purchased/ Received:

Tasting	Description

When:

Appearance:

Where:

Aroma:

With:

Body:

Overall Rating:

☆☆☆☆☆

Palate:

Recommend?

(YES) (NO)

Finish:

Additional Notes/Comments

Wine:

Vintage:

Grapes:

Type:

Region:

ABV:

Producer:

Serving Temp:

Pairs with:

Suggested Glass:

Price:	Purchased/Gift from:	Date Purchased/ Received:

Tasting

When:

Where:

With:

Overall Rating:

☆☆☆☆☆

Recommend?

YES   NO

Description

Appearance:

Aroma:

Body:

Palate:

Finish:

Additional Notes/Comments

Wine:

Vintage:

Grapes:

Type:

Region:

ABV:

Producer:

Serving Temp:

Pairs with:

Suggested Glass:

| Price: | Purchased/Gift from: | Date Purchased/Received: |

Tasting

When:

Where:

With:

Overall Rating:

☆☆☆☆☆

Recommend?

(YES) (NO)

Description

Appearance:

Aroma:

Body:

Palate:

Finish:

Additional Notes/Comments

Wine:

Vintage:

Grapes:

Type:

Region:

ABV:

Producer:

Serving Temp:

Pairs with:

Suggested Glass:

Price:	Purchased/Gift from:	Date Purchased/ Received:

Tasting

When:

Where:

With:

Overall Rating:

☆☆☆☆☆

Recommend?

YES   NO

Description

Appearance:

Aroma:

Body:

Palate:

Finish:

Additional Notes/Comments

Wine:

Vintage:

Grapes:

Type:

Region:

ABV:

Producer:

Serving Temp:

Pairs with:

Suggested Glass:

Price:	Purchased/Gift from:	Date Purchased/ Received:

Tasting

When:

Where:

With:

Overall Rating:

☆☆☆☆☆

Recommend?

YES   NO

Description

Appearance:

Aroma:

Body:

Palate:

Finish:

Additional Notes/Comments

Wine:

Vintage:

Grapes: _____

Type: _____

Region: _____

ABV: _____

Producer: _____

Serving Temp: _____

Pairs with: _____

Suggested Glass:

| Price: | Purchased/Gift from: | Date Purchased/Received: |

Tasting

When:
....
Where:
....
With:

Overall Rating:
☆☆☆☆☆

Recommend?
(YES)   (NO)

Description

Appearance: _____

Aroma: _____

Body: _____

Palate: _____

Finish: _____

Additional Notes/Comments

_____
_____
_____
_____
_____
_____
_____
_____
_____

Wine:

Vintage:

Grapes:

Type:

Region:

ABV:

Producer:

Serving Temp:

Pairs with:

Suggested Glass:

Price:	Purchased/Gift from:	Date Purchased/Received:

Tasting

When:

Where:

With:

Overall Rating:

☆☆☆☆☆

Recommend?

(YES) (NO)

Description

Appearance:

Aroma:

Body:

Palate:

Finish:

Additional Notes/Comments

Wine:

Vintage:

Grapes:

Type:

Region:

ABV:

Producer:

Serving Temp:

Pairs with:

Suggested Glass:

Price:	Purchased/Gift from:	Date Purchased/Received:

Tasting

When:

Where:

With:

Overall Rating:

☆☆☆☆☆

Recommend?

(YES)　(NO)

Description

Appearance:

Aroma:

Body:

Palate:

Finish:

Additional Notes/Comments

Wine:

Vintage:

Grapes:

Type:

Region:

ABV:

Producer:

Serving Temp:

Pairs with:

Suggested Glass:

| Price: | Purchased/Gift from: | Date Purchased/Received: |

Tasting

When:

Where:

With:

Overall Rating:

☆☆☆☆☆

Recommend?

YES   NO

Description

Appearance:

Aroma:

Body:

Palate:

Finish:

Additional Notes/Comments

Wine:

Vintage:

Grapes: _____

Type: _____

Region: _____

ABV: _____

Producer: _____

Serving Temp: _____

Pairs with: _____

Suggested Glass:

Price:	Purchased/Gift from:	Date Purchased/Received:

Tasting

When:

Where:

With:

Overall Rating:
☆☆☆☆☆

Recommend?
YES   NO

Description

Appearance: _____

Aroma: _____

Body: _____

Palate: _____

Finish: _____

Additional Notes/Comments

Wine:

Vintage:

Grapes:

Type:

Region:

ABV:

Producer:

Serving Temp:

Pairs with:

Suggested Glass:

Price:	Purchased/Gift from:	Date Purchased/ Received:

Tasting

When:

Where:

With:

Overall Rating:

☆☆☆☆☆

Recommend?

(YES) (NO)

Description

Appearance:

Aroma:

Body:

Palate:

Finish:

Additional Notes/Comments

Wine:

Vintage:

Grapes:

Type:

Region:

ABV:

Producer:

Serving Temp:

Pairs with:

Suggested Glass:

Price:	Purchased/Gift from:	Date Purchased/ Received:

Tasting

When:

Where:

With:

Overall Rating:

☆☆☆☆☆

Recommend?

YES   NO

Description

Appearance:

Aroma:

Body:

Palate:

Finish:

Additional Notes/Comments

Wine:

Vintage:

Grapes:

Type:

Region:

ABV:

Producer:

Serving Temp:

Pairs with:

Suggested Glass:

Price:	Purchased/Gift from:	Date Purchased/ Received:

Tasting

When:

Where:

With:

Overall Rating:

☆☆☆☆☆

Recommend?

YES   NO

Description

Appearance:

Aroma:

Body:

Palate:

Finish:

Additional Notes/Comments

Wine:

Vintage:

Grapes:

Type:

Region:

ABV:

Producer:

Serving Temp:

Pairs with:

Suggested Glass:

Price:	Purchased/Gift from:	Date Purchased/ Received:

Tasting

When:

Where:

With:

Overall Rating:

☆☆☆☆☆

Recommend?

(YES) (NO)

Description

Appearance:

Aroma:

Body:

Palate:

Finish:

Additional Notes/Comments

Wine:

Vintage:

Grapes:

Type:

Region:

ABV:

Producer:

Serving Temp:

Pairs with:

Suggested Glass:

Price:	Purchased/Gift from:	Date Purchased/Received:

Tasting

When:

Where:

With:

Overall Rating:

☆☆☆☆☆

Recommend?

YES   NO

Description

Appearance:

Aroma:

Body:

Palate:

Finish:

Additional Notes/Comments

Wine:

Vintage:

Grapes: _____

Type: _____

Region: _____

ABV: _____

Producer: _____

Serving Temp: _____

Pairs with: _____

Suggested Glass:

Price:	Purchased/Gift from:	Date Purchased/ Received:

Tasting

When:

Where:

With:

Overall Rating:
☆☆☆☆☆

Recommend?
(YES)   (NO)

Description

Appearance: _____

Aroma: _____

Body: _____

Palate: _____

Finish: _____

Additional Notes/Comments

_____
_____
_____
_____
_____
_____
_____
_____

Wine:

Vintage:

Grapes: _____

Type: _____

Region: _____

ABV: _____

Producer: _____

Serving Temp: _____

Pairs with: _____

Suggested Glass:

Price:	Purchased/Gift from:	Date Purchased/Received:

Tasting

When:

Where:

With:

Overall Rating:

☆☆☆☆☆

Recommend?

(YES)   (NO)

Description

Appearance: _____

Aroma: _____

Body: _____

Palate: _____

Finish: _____

Additional Notes/Comments

_____
_____
_____
_____
_____
_____
_____
_____
_____

Wine:

Vintage:

Grapes:

Type:

Region:

ABV:

Producer:

Serving Temp:

Pairs with:

Suggested Glass:

Price:	Purchased/Gift from:	Date Purchased/Received:

Tasting

When:

Where:

With:

Overall Rating:

☆☆☆☆☆

Recommend?

(YES) (NO)

Description

Appearance:

Aroma:

Body:

Palate:

Finish:

Additional Notes/Comments

Wine:

Vintage:

Grapes: _____

Type: _____

Region: _____

ABV: _____

Producer: _____

Serving Temp: _____

Pairs with: _____

Suggested Glass: _____

Price:	Purchased/Gift from:	Date Purchased/Received:

Tasting

When:

Where:

With:

Overall Rating:

☆☆☆☆☆

Recommend?

YES NO

Description

Appearance: _____

Aroma: _____

Body: _____

Palate: _____

Finish: _____

Additional Notes/Comments

_____
_____
_____
_____
_____
_____
_____
_____
_____

Wine:

Vintage:

Grapes:

Type:

Region:

ABV:

Producer:

Serving Temp:

Pairs with:

Suggested Glass:

Price:	Purchased/Gift from:	Date Purchased/ Received:

Tasting

When:

Where:

With:

Overall Rating:

☆☆☆☆☆

Recommend?

(YES)   (NO)

Description

Appearance:

Aroma:

Body:

Palate:

Finish:

Additional Notes/Comments

Wine:

Vintage:

Grapes: _____

Type: _____

Region: _____

ABV: _____

Producer: _____

Serving Temp: _____

Pairs with: _____

Suggested Glass:

Price:	Purchased/Gift from:	Date Purchased/ Received:

Tasting

When:

Where:

With:

Overall Rating:

☆☆☆☆☆

Recommend?

(YES) (NO)

Description

Appearance: _____

Aroma: _____

Body: _____

Palate: _____

Finish: _____

Additional Notes/Comments

_____
_____
_____
_____
_____
_____
_____
_____
_____

Wine:

Vintage:

Grapes:

Type:

Region:

ABV:

Producer:

Serving Temp:

Pairs with:

Suggested Glass:

Price:	Purchased/Gift from:	Date Purchased/ Received:

Tasting

When:

Where:

With:

Overall Rating:

☆☆☆☆☆

Recommend?

YES NO

Description

Appearance:

Aroma:

Body:

Palate:

Finish:

Additional Notes/Comments

Wine:

Vintage:

Grapes: _____

Type: _____

Region: _____

ABV: _____

Producer: _____

Serving Temp: _____

Pairs with: _____

Suggested Glass: _____

Price:	Purchased/Gift from:	Date Purchased/Received:

Tasting

When: _____

Where: _____

With: _____

Overall Rating:

☆☆☆☆☆

Recommend?

(YES)   (NO)

Description

Appearance: _____

Aroma: _____

Body: _____

Palate: _____

Finish: _____

Additional Notes/Comments

_____
_____
_____
_____
_____
_____
_____
_____

Wine:

Vintage:

Grapes: _____

Type: _____

Region: _____

ABV: _____

Producer: _____

Serving Temp: _____

Pairs with: _____

Suggested Glass: _____

Price:	Purchased/Gift from:	Date Purchased/ Received:

Tasting

When:

....

Where:

....

With:

Overall Rating:

☆☆☆☆☆

Recommend?

(YES) (NO)

Description

Appearance: _____

_____

Aroma: _____

_____

Body: _____

_____

Palate: _____

_____

Finish: _____

_____

Additional Notes/Comments

_____
_____
_____
_____
_____
_____
_____
_____
_____

Wine:

Vintage:

Grapes: _____

Type: _____

Region: _____

ABV: _____

Producer: _____

Serving Temp: _____

Pairs with: _____

Suggested Glass:

Price:	Purchased/Gift from:	Date Purchased/ Received:

Tasting

When:

Where:

With:

Overall Rating:

☆☆☆☆☆

Recommend?

(YES)   (NO)

Description

Appearance: _____

Aroma: _____

Body: _____

Palate: _____

Finish: _____

Additional Notes/Comments

_____
_____
_____
_____
_____
_____
_____
_____
_____

Wine:

Vintage:

Grapes:

Type:

Region:

ABV:

Producer:

Serving Temp:

Pairs with:

Suggested Glass:

Price:	Purchased/Gift from:	Date Purchased/Received:

Tasting

When:

Where:

With:

Overall Rating:

☆☆☆☆☆

Recommend?

(YES)   (NO)

Description

Appearance:

Aroma:

Body:

Palate:

Finish:

Additional Notes/Comments

Wine:

Vintage:

Grapes:

Type:

Region:

ABV:

Producer:

Serving Temp:

Pairs with:

Suggested Glass:

Price:	Purchased/Gift from:	Date Purchased/Received:

Tasting

When:

Where:

With:

Overall Rating:

☆☆☆☆☆

Recommend?

YES   NO

Description

Appearance:

Aroma:

Body:

Palate:

Finish:

Additional Notes/Comments

Wine:

Vintage:

Grapes: _____

Type: _____

Region: _____

ABV: _____

Producer: _____

Serving Temp: _____

Pairs with: _____

Suggested Glass:

Price:	Purchased/Gift from:	Date Purchased/Received:

Tasting

When:

Where:

With:

Overall Rating:

☆☆☆☆☆

Recommend?

(YES)   (NO)

Description

Appearance: _____

Aroma: _____

Body: _____

Palate: _____

Finish: _____

Additional Notes/Comments

_____
_____
_____
_____
_____
_____
_____
_____

Wine:

Vintage:

Grapes:

Type:

Region:

ABV:

Producer:

Serving Temp:

Pairs with:

Suggested Glass:

Price:	Purchased/Gift from:	Date Purchased/Received:

Tasting

When:

Where:

With:

Overall Rating:

☆☆☆☆☆

Recommend?

YES   NO

Description

Appearance:

Aroma:

Body:

Palate:

Finish:

Additional Notes/Comments

Wine:

Vintage:

Grapes: _____

Type: _____

Region: _____

ABV: _____

Producer: _____

Serving Temp: _____

Pairs with: _____

Suggested Glass:

Price:	Purchased/Gift from:	Date Purchased/Received:

Tasting

When: _____

Where: _____

With: _____

Overall Rating:
☆☆☆☆☆

Recommend?
YES   NO

Description

Appearance: _____

Aroma: _____

Body: _____

Palate: _____

Finish: _____

Additional Notes/Comments

_____
_____
_____
_____
_____
_____
_____
_____

Wine:

Vintage:

Grapes:

Type:

Region:

ABV:

Producer:

Serving Temp:

Pairs with:

Suggested Glass:

Price:	Purchased/Gift from:	Date Purchased/ Received:

Tasting

When:

Where:

With:

Overall Rating:

☆☆☆☆☆

Recommend?

YES   NO

Description

Appearance:

Aroma:

Body:

Palate:

Finish:

Additional Notes/Comments

Wine:

Vintage:

Grapes:

Type:

Region:

ABV:

Producer:

Serving Temp:

Pairs with:

Suggested Glass:

| Price: | Purchased/Gift from: | Date Purchased/Received: |

Tasting

When:

Where:

With:

Overall Rating:

☆☆☆☆☆

Recommend?

YES   NO

Description

Appearance:

Aroma:

Body:

Palate:

Finish:

Additional Notes/Comments

Wine:

Vintage:

Grapes: _____

Type: _____

Region: _____

ABV: _____

Producer: _____

Serving Temp: _____

Pairs with: _____

Suggested Glass:

Price:	Purchased/Gift from:	Date Purchased/ Received:

Tasting

When: _____

Where: _____

With: _____

Overall Rating:

☆☆☆☆☆

Recommend?

(YES)   (NO)

Description

Appearance: _____

Aroma: _____

Body: _____

Palate: _____

Finish: _____

Additional Notes/Comments

_____
_____
_____
_____
_____
_____
_____
_____
_____

Wine:

Vintage:

Grapes:

Type:

Region:

ABV:

Producer:

Serving Temp:

Pairs with:

Suggested Glass:

Price:	Purchased/Gift from:	Date Purchased/Received:

Tasting

When:

Where:

With:

Overall Rating:

☆☆☆☆☆

Recommend?

YES   NO

Description

Appearance:

Aroma:

Body:

Palate:

Finish:

Additional Notes/Comments

Wine:

Vintage:

Grapes:

Type:

Region:

ABV:

Producer:

Serving Temp:

Pairs with:

Suggested Glass:

Price:	Purchased/Gift from:	Date Purchased/ Received:

Tasting

When:

Where:

With:

Overall Rating:

☆☆☆☆☆

Recommend?

YES   NO

Description

Appearance:

Aroma:

Body:

Palate:

Finish:

Additional Notes/Comments

Wine:

Vintage:

Grapes:

Type:

Region:

ABV:

Producer:

Serving Temp:

Pairs with:

Suggested Glass:

Price:	Purchased/Gift from:	Date Purchased/Received:

Tasting

When:

Where:

With:

Overall Rating:

☆☆☆☆☆

Recommend?

YES   NO

Description

Appearance:

Aroma:

Body:

Palate:

Finish:

Additional Notes/Comments

Wine:

Vintage:

Grapes: _____

Type: _____

Region: _____

ABV: _____

Producer: _____

Serving Temp: _____

Pairs with: _____

Suggested Glass:

Price:	Purchased/Gift from:	Date Purchased/Received:

Tasting

When:

Where:

With:

Overall Rating:
☆☆☆☆☆

Recommend?
(YES) (NO)

Description

Appearance: _____

Aroma: _____

Body: _____

Palate: _____

Finish: _____

Additional Notes/Comments

_____
_____
_____
_____
_____
_____
_____
_____
_____

Wine:

Vintage:

Grapes:

Type:

Region:

ABV:

Producer:

Serving Temp:

Pairs with:

Suggested Glass:

Price:	Purchased/Gift from:	Date Purchased/Received:

Tasting

When:

Where:

With:

Overall Rating:

☆☆☆☆☆

Recommend?

YES   NO

Description

Appearance:

Aroma:

Body:

Palate:

Finish:

Additional Notes/Comments

Wine:

Vintage:

Grapes:

Type:

Region:

ABV:

Producer:

Serving Temp:

Pairs with:

Suggested Glass:

Price:	Purchased/Gift from:	Date Purchased/ Received:

Tasting

When:

Where:

With:

Overall Rating:

☆☆☆☆☆

Recommend?

(YES) (NO)

Description

Appearance:

Aroma:

Body:

Palate:

Finish:

Additional Notes/Comments

Wine:

Vintage:

Grapes:

Type:

Region:

ABV:

Producer:

Serving Temp:

Pairs with:

Suggested Glass:

Price:	Purchased/Gift from:	Date Purchased/Received:

Tasting

When:

Where:

With:

Overall Rating:

☆☆☆☆☆

Recommend?

(YES) (NO)

Description

Appearance:

Aroma:

Body:

Palate:

Finish:

Additional Notes/Comments

Wine:

Vintage:

Grapes: _____

Type: _____

Region: _____

ABV: _____

Producer: _____

Serving Temp: _____

Pairs with: _____

Suggested Glass:

Price:	Purchased/Gift from:	Date Purchased/Received:

Tasting

When:

Where:

With:

Overall Rating:

☆☆☆☆☆

Recommend?

YES   NO

Description

Appearance: _____

Aroma: _____

Body: _____

Palate: _____

Finish: _____

Additional Notes/Comments

_____
_____
_____
_____
_____
_____
_____
_____

Wine:

Vintage:

Grapes:

Type:

Region:

ABV:

Producer:

Serving Temp:

Pairs with:

Suggested Glass:

Price:	Purchased/Gift from:	Date Purchased/ Received:

Tasting

When:

Where:

With:

Overall Rating:

☆☆☆☆☆

Recommend?

YES   NO

Description

Appearance:

Aroma:

Body:

Palate:

Finish:

Additional Notes/Comments

Wine:

Vintage:

Grapes:

Type:

Region:

ABV:

Producer:

Serving Temp:

Pairs with:

Suggested Glass:

Price:	Purchased/Gift from:	Date Purchased/ Received:

Tasting

When:

Where:

With:

Overall Rating:

☆☆☆☆☆

Recommend?

(YES) (NO)

Description

Appearance:

Aroma:

Body:

Palate:

Finish:

Additional Notes/Comments

Wine:

Vintage:

Grapes:

Type:

Region:

ABV:

Producer:

Serving Temp:

Pairs with:

Suggested Glass:

Price:	Purchased/Gift from:	Date Purchased/Received:

Tasting

When:

Where:

With:

Overall Rating:

☆☆☆☆☆

Recommend?

YES   NO

Description

Appearance:

Aroma:

Body:

Palate:

Finish:

Additional Notes/Comments

Wine:

Vintage:

Grapes:

Type:

Region:

ABV:

Producer:

Serving Temp:

Pairs with:

Suggested Glass:

Price:	Purchased/Gift from:	Date Purchased/ Received:

Tasting

When:

Where:

With:

Overall Rating:

☆☆☆☆☆

Recommend?

YES   NO

Description

Appearance:

Aroma:

Body:

Palate:

Finish:

Additional Notes/Comments

Wine:

Vintage:

Grapes:

Type:

Region:

ABV:

Producer:

Serving Temp:

Pairs with:

Suggested Glass:

Price:	Purchased/Gift from:	Date Purchased/ Received:

Tasting

When:

Where:

With:

Overall Rating:

☆☆☆☆☆

Recommend?

(YES)   (NO)

Description

Appearance:

Aroma:

Body:

Palate:

Finish:

Additional Notes/Comments

Wine:

Vintage:

Grapes:

Type:

Region:

ABV:

Producer:

Serving Temp:

Pairs with:

Suggested Glass:

| Price: | Purchased/Gift from: | Date Purchased/Received: |

Tasting

When:

Where:

With:

Overall Rating:

☆☆☆☆☆

Recommend?

YES   NO

Description

Appearance:

Aroma:

Body:

Palate:

Finish:

Additional Notes/Comments

Wine:

Vintage:

Grapes:

Type:

Region:

ABV:

Producer:

Serving Temp:

Pairs with:

Suggested Glass:

Price:	Purchased/Gift from:	Date Purchased/Received:

Tasting

When:

Where:

With:

Overall Rating:

☆☆☆☆☆

Recommend?

(YES) (NO)

Description

Appearance:

Aroma:

Body:

Palate:

Finish:

Additional Notes/Comments

Wine:

Vintage:

Grapes: _____

Type: _____

Region: _____

ABV: _____

Producer: _____

Serving Temp: _____

Pairs with: _____

Suggested Glass:

Price:	Purchased/Gift from:	Date Purchased/ Received:

Tasting

When:

Where:

With:

Overall Rating:

☆☆☆☆☆

Recommend?

(YES) (NO)

Description

Appearance: _____

Aroma: _____

Body: _____

Palate: _____

Finish: _____

Additional Notes/Comments

_____
_____
_____
_____
_____
_____
_____
_____
_____

Wine:

Vintage:

Grapes:

Type:

Region:

ABV:

Producer:

Serving Temp:

Pairs with:

Suggested Glass:

Price:	Purchased/Gift from:	Date Purchased/ Received:

Tasting

When:

Where:

With:

Overall Rating:

☆☆☆☆☆

Recommend?

YES   NO

Description

Appearance:

Aroma:

Body:

Palate:

Finish:

Additional Notes/Comments

Wine:

Vintage:

Grapes:

Type:

Region:

ABV:

Producer:

Serving Temp:

Pairs with:

Suggested Glass:

Price:	Purchased/Gift from:	Date Purchased/Received:

Tasting

When:

Where:

With:

Overall Rating:

☆☆☆☆☆

Recommend?

YES   NO

Description

Appearance:

Aroma:

Body:

Palate:

Finish:

Additional Notes/Comments